Language (PHP)

PHP has many features that make it the perfe   ⌐ ᴜevelopers
in the world:

Easy

PHP is one of the easiest to learn programming languages, it relieves you of
all the complexities of memory management and the complexities of word
processing in C on the one hand, and a lot of weakness in the interface and
design of the programming language Perl on the other.

PHP has a very straightforward structure and rules.Most grammar is taken
from C, Java, and Perl to create a very easy and smooth programming
language without losing any power in the language.This is useful if you
learn anything about other programming languages like Visual Basic or C or
Java where you will always find that you understand the course materials
quickly, and you will discover how PHP facilitates the most difficult things
and humiliates the obstacles facing the programmer to devote himself
completely to creativity, everything you think you can do in PHP language.

the speed

PHP is a well-known language for high-speed implementation of programs,
especially in the fourth version of the translator, where the PHP translator
was written from scratch to give great performance, and PHP language is
originally designed as a kernel of the translator, so that you can put this
kernel in several templates or To work with different technologies, you can
run a PHP compiler such as a CGI program, but it is best to install the PHP
compiler on an IIS server as an additional module that is added to the
server via ISAPI functions, and another version is installed on the Apache
server as an external module. There is also a customized version to
integrate with Apache server code to become part of Apache PHS, which is

now the most used method in web servers running on UNIX systems and is the way that gives the best performance for the PHP interpreter, where the translator becomes part of the provider, and therefore it will be loaded in memory waiting for PHP pages to translate and display them directly to visitors without the additional delay required Perl / CGI programs, for example, have to run a Perl compiler with each page visit to translate the page, then close the compiler, then call it back on the second visit, and so on.This makes a big difference in high-pressure sites in particular, and using PHP is a much better solution.

Advantages

The PHP compiler comes loaded with a huge number of ready-to-use functions in all fields, from mathematical and computational processing functions to database access functions and FTP servers. For example, PHP functions provide access to MySQL, PostgreSQL, MS SQL, Oracle and other database servers. There are also a set of functions to process XML files, and other functions to send and receive files remotely using FTP, and a set of functions to process and produce images dynamically and Flash files dynamically, not to mention all functions for word processing and arrays.

Interoperability

As we said earlier, although there are a lot of PHP versions that each work in a different environment, they all share the original kernel that actually processes PHP files, so all PHP interpreters behave the same way with scripts. What I've done is running on Windows with IIS provider, it should work without any changes when you move it to Apache, of course, some things are very simple provided by some servers without others, but all the programs that I have written since I began to learn the language so far works on all Servers without the need for any changes, in addition to that Very few changes have occurred in the basic language from the third to the fourth version, and most of the changes have been in the translator's infrastructure.

Protection

PHP provides a lot of advanced features, but it provides you with the appropriate ways to set limits on these features, you can control the number of allowed connections to the database, for example, the maximum size of files that can be sent via the browser, or allow the use of some features or cancellation of use, all this Via a PHP configuration file controlled by the site administrator.

Scalability

You can easily expand the PHP compiler and add the features you want to it in C. Since the compiler code is open, you can change what you want directly to get the version that suits you best, and you can also create additional modules that are installed on the compiler to increase its features and functions. The PHP compiler development team has already done this task and converted a huge amount of C libraries into custom libraries to be added to the compiler, from which we got all the features we talked about like accessing databases and processing XML files.

History of PHP

PHP started as a library of functions added to the Perl language to make CGI programs easier in Perl. Perl miniature with some additional features of the Web, and then added to the support for HTML forms and called PHP2 / FI, a group of programmers worked on the PHP interpreter and added an application programming interface API to facilitate the process of

PHP 3, after a period of time Zend Technologies The
age translator, also called zend, has been
_peed Combined with other PHP libraries to create
..e PHP compiler, the PHP compiler is now divided into two
..ie zend compiler is developed on CVS servers located in the zend
site and the second section is called PHP which is the basic libraries and
functions that come with the program, the zend compiler PHP now
contains libraries written in C language and compatible with the application
interface provided by the zend compiler, so the two sections work together
to create a PHP interpreter, and when you visit the official PHP site now
and get PHP Translator Or a code you get your code, you get both the
compiler and libraries zend PHP together.

PHP is a surprising development in recent times, and statistically Net Craft
indicates that the PHP interpreter is the most popular Apache provider on
the Internet, and that the PHP interpreter is installed on about two million
web providers on the Internet.

The structure of PHP files

PHP files are simple text files, similar in structure to ASP files and HTML
files in general, PHP file consists of two sections, the HTML section and PHP
section, the file is normally a normal HTML file, but you can specify certain
parts of the file where the file out of HTML To PHP mode, to output the file
to PHP mode there are several ways:

1- Using the <? Php and?> Tags is as follows:

```
<? php

echo 'This is PHP output!';

?>
```

2 - Use the manual pair. It is used in the same way as before, but without the word php in the start tag. This type of tag requires less typing, of course, but it conflicts with the xml tags, so some people close the short tag feature so that this conflict does not occur (you can close This feature is easily via the PHP settings file).

3 - Using the ASP tag pair, which is named as the pair of tags used in ASP files (<% and%>), the feature of the ASP tags is not standard, but you can activate it via the PHP compiler settings file.

4 - The last method is to use the following tag pair:

```php
<script language = "php">
echo 'This is PHP output!';
</script>
```

However, this method is not currently used, as it makes it difficult to distinguish between PHP codes and the rest of the HTML file, as well as for programs that write HTML files that give color to the code, most of them do not recognize this type of code and consider it part of the normal HTML file.

The best way to switch to PHP mode is to use the first tag pair of course, since it is the most used one, it does not contain any conflicts and it works on all PHP interpreters whatever their settings, which is why we will use them in all the examples that you will find in this course.

Write PHP files

PHP files are simple text files just like HTML files. You can write PHP script in any text-writing program that allows you to write simple text files Plain

Text like Notepad on Windows, but the majority of PHP programmers use other tools that make it easier for them to programming by coloring the code , Making it easier to search for files and replace sections from multiple files at the same time, such as HomeSite.Although you won't need many of these features, using Notepad to make PHP files is very difficult, especially in large files since Notepad doesn't allow Open large files, the biggest problem is that they do not provide v If you get the error message indicating an error on line 53, you will not be able to know the required line in Notepad unless you manually count from the first line to 53. Well what if the error is in line 652, you can start typing your script in the program now available Until you get another program, you can, of course, open your files in any text editor.

To create a PHP file now, open the text editor of your choice, start typing the page you want, don't forget to enclose the PHP code with its tags, then save the file anywhere in your web directory and give it the appropriate .php or .php3 extension depending on your server settings. Visit the page using your browser and you'll find the page translated and displayed to you.

Remember that you must visit the page through your web provider, and you cannot view the page by opening it as an external file, for example, if the root directory of your provider's pages is: C: \ httpd \

And you created a page I called test.php in that directory, you should now run the web server and visit the page at http: //localhost/test.php, if you use the Open command from the File menu in your browser to open the file C: \ httpd \ test .php you will not see a translated PHP page, and you will see only PHP code.

Training

Execute the following PHP file:

```
This is the normal html page. <br>
<? php
echo "This is inside PHP <br>";
echo "Hello World! <br>";
?>
```

What do you see when you run the previous program? You should see the following output:

This is the normal html page.

This is inside PHP

Hello World!

Now that you have finished writing your first program in PHP, do not worry if you do not understand anything in it, we will now learn how to use variables and phrases in PHP.

Let's write a simple script (appetizer):

```
<html dir = "rtl">
Hi
<?
("How are you") Echo
?>
</html>
```

Save the file as echo.php

We will be presented with a phrase written in it

Hi

How are you doing

It's simple, isn't it?

The php code consists of text, code, tags and html language and may not contain html texts.

In order for the code to work, it must be a php file extension or any other php file extension

For example, php3 and phtml

- Hey.

When you request a page on the Internet, you make a direct connection to the server. This process is called request to the server. Return to it and compile (compile) to become a valid page to display this process, which happened similar to the theory of the client to the server (client to server) so that the browser is the client and the server is the server.

The server stores, translates and distributes the data while the client (your web browser) passes to the server and gets the data

Internet Protocols:

We do not want to go here to talk about the history of the ancient Internet, the important point is the network linked to the Internet nodes designed to preserve information to be transferred from one place to another and uses a set of protocols such as Tcp / Ip in order to transfer data over the network.

Tcp / Ip protocol

One of the advantages of this protocol is that it can reboot its way to data if it is faulty at a point or place during the transfer and this is done very quickly. When the user asks the browser to bring him a page from the Internet, the browser fetches these commands using a protocol called this protocol TCP A protocol is a data transfer protocol that ensures that data is sent and accessed correctly.

Before the data is sent over the network it must be addressed and the protocol that addresses the data is called HTTP. This protocol addresses the data so that TCP knows where it will transfer data (it cannot transfer data if it has no purpose or place). When you see the page followed by http: //, you know directly that the Internet uses the HTTP protocol to bring this page. You can take a picture that TCP is a postman who delivers a message.

The request is passed from the browser to the web server or server, which is known as HTTP request and the server sees its data repository in order to get the required data. If the page is found in the repository, it is sent in packets to the requesting party using the TCP protocol. Using the http protocol (always be aware that it sends them in packets so you know why when a complete web page does not appear that a packet was not sent well) but if the server does not find the requested page it sends a page containing a 404 error message and this page sent from Web server to the supernova You have an HTTP response.

HTTP protocol

Although we have taken a lot of information and many stories similar to the stories of a thousand nights or tales of children, but we still miss a lot of details in this subject so let's dive a little in the details about the HTTP protocol in particular.

When you make a request for a page from the server, additional things are sent along with the request request, other than the URL, which is sent as part of the http request.

Same topic with http response There are other things linking with him as part of it.

Much of this information is automatically generated in the HTTP message and the user will not deal with it directly, so you do not need to worry about this information if you did not create it in the first place. Gives us additional control over this information.

All HTTP messages take a specific format, either Request or Response. We can divide this format into three sections:

1 - Request / response line

2 - Http header

3 - Http body

The content of these three things depends on the type of message if it is HTTp Request or HTTP response so we will talk about them in more depth.

Http Request

The request must contain at least the request line and the HOST.

Your Internet browser sends an HTTP request to the Web server that contains the following:

1- The Request Line

The first line of each request (http request) is the Request Line, which contains three types of information:

A - HTTP command, which means method.

B - the path from the server to the required resources (web pages) required by the client (browser)

C - HTTP version.

So as an example of the Request Line look at the following line:

GET /testpage.htm HTTP / 1.1

The method tells the server how to handle the request. There are three common types of method

- HTTP Header

The second bit of information is the HTTP header, which contains details or documentation about the client, such as the type of browser (Netscape or Explorer) that requested the page, time, date, and general settings.

The HTTP Header contains information that we can divide into three categories:

A - GENERAL: Contains information about either the client or the server and does not specialize to an individual or group.

B - Entity: contains information about the data sent between the browser and the server.

C) Request: Contains data on the client's settings and the various types of data accepted.

Here's an example:

Accept: * / *

Accept language: Arabic-KSA.

Connection: Keep –Alive.

Host: http://www.arabbuielder.com

Referer: http://www.arabbuielder.com/index.php?something=132

User –Agent: Iexploer (win98; ....)

As you can see the HTTP Header is a setup consisting of several lines, each line contains certain values.

There are several lines that make up the HTTP header and most of them are optional. HTTP reports the expiration of the header information by leaving a blank line (this is in HTTP1.1).

3- The HTTP Body:

If the POST command is used in the HTTP Request Line, then HTTP requests the information sent in the body to the server.

Http Response

Sends from the server to the browser and contains three things:

1- the Response Line

2 - http header

3 - Http Body

1 - The Response Line

The response line contains only two types of information:

1 - HTTP version number.

2 - The code or http request code that determines if the request is successful or failed.

Example :

HTTP / 1.1 200 OK

In this example, the response line returns the value 200, followed by the word OK, which indicates the success of the request and the response contains the requested page and data from the server. Another example is code 404 when you request a page and the server fails to get it.

2 - HTTP Header

The response header is similar to the request hader discussed above. The information in it is also divided into three types:

A - GENERAL: Information about the client or server and not to one of them.

B - Entity: contains information about the data that is sent between the server and the client.

Answer: Response: Contains information about the server that sent the response and how it handles and processes the response (Response).

As we said earlier, it consists of several lines and a blank line is placed to inform the end of the hyd.

Example :

HTTP / 1.1 200 OK -the satus line

Date: Mon; 1st Nov 1999, 16:12:23 GMT -general header

Server: Apache / 1.3.12 (Unix) (SUSE / Linux) PHP / 4.0.2 -the response

Last-modified: Fri, 29 Oct 1999, 12:08:03 GMT -Entity Header

The first line we discussed and the second line is understood without explanation, the third line identifies the program according to the server and its type and operating system and the last line defines the last time the page was modified or refreshed.

Note: Hydr may contain more than this information or different information depending on the type of thing required from the server.

3 - Http Body

If the request is processed successfully, the HTTP response Body contains the HTML code and the web browser interprets it and converts it to the final page you see.

Where is the PHP script from all this?

We now have a good concept of how the browser sends a page request from the server and how the server responds to that request.

We talked about that the php script consists of three things: text and php code and html code, we can not describe html as a good programming language and we can say that php Scripting Language because it adds html capabilities on them such as tables and frames in html code inside the php code There are languages called languages Scripts that you may be familiar with, such as JavaScript and Fajol Basic Script, except that the difference between them and php is that php is a language dependent on the provider, ie the server and you can customize the browser that browses.

The html makes us guarantee that the php scripts are within the rules so that we can run them, but we do not forget that the extension of the files remains as php or php3 unchanged so that the script is sent to the translation library (scripting engine) which translates the script to html (as if translated from Arabic to English or Conversely)

The concept of parsing and Execution:

We can divide the translation process done by the php server into two or two operations:

The first process is that the server first checks the grammar and this does not guarantee that the script is 100 percent correct, but it checks the commands and grammar and this is what they call Parsing

The second process is to execute the script and then output it in the form of html code and this is called the Execution.

It remains to be known that scripts are of two types:

1 - which is implemented by the provider

Server –Side scripting

2 - implemented by the browser (Internet page).

Comments

What do you think if you are in a company and have more than one programmer and you want to design a program, then you may need to organize and modify the work so it is necessary to make a clarification of the usefulness of the code you wrote in order to make it easier to understand them and add appropriate modifications, then comments are used to explain the codes Information is only used as an illustration or anything else.

You can make a one-line comment like this:

```
<?

"This is a comment that has no meaning

?>
```

Another example :

```
<?

// This function prints a comment word

"Comment";

?>
```

Also you can use a comment from more than one line as follows:

```
<?
```

/ * Comment consists of

More than one line with a slash mark and a star

* /

?>

Variables

What are the variables?

The simplest definition we can say about a variable is that it is a space of memory used to store information and controlled by the programmer in PHP, the variables start with the $ sign and to enter a value in the variable you use the parameter (=) So to create a variable that contains a value Do this as follows:

$ alfares = "How Are You Every Body?";

$ Variable_name = value;

Note that the previous line consists of five things:

1 / The variable is alfares

2 / before the $ sign so that the PHP interpreter knows that it is a variable

3 / Modulus (=)

4 / semicolon (;)

5 / The value is How Are You Every Body? It is the value in the variable or that we suggested for the variable or that we put in it (because the value suggested is you (php programmer))

Notes :

1. Variable names are case sensitive if they are uppercase and lowercase

```
<?
$ Ahmed = "salem";
$ ahmed = "slmoon";
echo $ ahmed;
echo $ Ahmed;
?>
```

The two variables above are different because of the case.

2 - You can use the operator (_)
$ First_name

3 - You can use a thousand characters in naming variables (in fact they are undefined).

Quotations marks

 An important point is why we put these quotes? The answer is that the value that we set literal consists of texts and there are types of variables and so we will separate and say

There are data types:

1 - strings (letters)

$ Exa = "Just An Example";

$ Exa2 = "2.5";

$ Exa3 = "2";

2 - Integer (numbers)

$ Exam = 5;

3 - Double (comma numbers)

$ num = 5.4

4 - array

Come later

5 - objects

Detailed in other lessons

6 - Unknown.

Come in another lesson.

Variables are not defined by the programmer, but the PHP interpreter recognizes them in order to complete different operations on them.

Data literal /

In PHP, any value that is between two regular quotes or a single quotation mark is considered by the PHP to be a literal value

Examples:

"This text is in plain quotes or double quotes"

'This text is in single or single quotation marks'

The text must start and end with the same quotation mark, otherwise PHP will not recognize the literal value or the text.

```
<?
$ d = "Mistake'
"error"
?>
```

You cannot also place a quotation mark of the same type as the literal value in the middle of the literal statement or text

```
<?
$ variable = "This text is a letter 'cause there is a tag in the text of the same type'";
?>
```

And correct it

```
<?
$ variable = "' true' this text ";
?>
```

And also another example

```
<?
$ r = "This is" BAD "; // Error
$ t = "This is' good "; // True
?>
```

If you insist on this or need it in the necessary processes (as we will see later in our need for modeling), you can put a parameter (\) before the quotation mark.

To work with you with ease.

Example :

```
<?
$ u = "This Only An \" Example \ "To Make You Understand Nothing";
?>
```

Ok what do you think if we want to print the operand (\) himself?
The solution is to follow it by its example.

```
$ file = "c: \ windows \ system.ini";
```

echo $ file; // Result c: windowssystem.ini

$ file = "c: \\ windows \\ system.ini";

echo $ file; // Result c: \ windows \ system.ini

You can combine the most variable values into one variable by the (.)

```
<?
$ first = "Forum";
$ last = "US Developer";
$ fullname = $ first. $ last
Echo $ fullname;
// But we want to put a space between the two words
$ fullname = $ first. ". $ last;
Echo $ fullname;
?>
```

And also we can guest to another value variable variable:

```php
<?
$ f = "I Love M";
$ k = "y Country";
// Add the value to the variable
$ f = $ f. $ k;
echo $ f;
?>
```

```php
<?
// Almost the same process
 $ f = "I Love M";
$ k = "y Country";
$ f. = $ k;
echo $ f;
?>
```

Numbers

Single and double number

The difference I have known so far is that the difference between them is the floating point (God even giving it this name makes one feel frustrated and afraid)

Note that we do not use quotation marks to define PHP as numeric data that we may use in complex calculations and we can apply simple calculations to them if they are literal.

// That's an odd number

$ j = 2

// That's a double number

$ h = 4.5

mathematical calculations

It is like addition, subtraction, multiplication and division and is arranged as follows:

First / parentheses

Second / multiplication and then divide.

Third / subtraction and addition

```
<?
Echo 5 * 2/5;
Echo 5 * (2/5);
```

```
?>
```

Another example :

```
<?
Echo 5-6 + 9;
?>
```

An example of a calculation where we use a literal variable

```
<?
$ W = "2L";
$ E = 2;
$ F = $ W * $ E;
echo $ W. ' '. $ E.' '. $ F;
?>
```

Example of another operation but it did not work and you must devise the reason yourself (huh Tal Zain):

```
<?
$ W = "L10";
$ E = 2;
$ F = $ W * $ E;
echo $ W. ".. $ E. " '. $ F;
?>
```

We can add one number to a variable in three different ways:

Example

$ j ++

or

$ j = $ j + 1

or

$ j + = 1

We can add this variable to itself as follows:

$ j + = $ j

Or as follows:

$ j = $ j + $ j

System variables

There are variables used by the system that you can use and from

$ HTTP_USER_AGENT

You appear to have the type of browser that the client is using

Example :

<?

Echo $ HTTP_USER_AGENT;

?>

Constants

We can define constants by saying that they are constant values and are defined by the define function

Constants are also case sensitive

```
<?
Define ("author", "alfarees");
Echo "author is". author;
?>
```

There are constants used by the system such as

PHP_OS

That displays the operating system that the server uses

Example :

```
<?
Echo PHP_OS;
?>
```

Know and convert data types

If you want to know what type of variable you can use the gettype function

Example :

```
<?
$ n = 5;
$ l = "hi";
echo "The n Is". gettype ($ n). "<br>";
echo "The l is". gettype ($ l);
?>
```

If you want to convert a variable type, you can do this by using the settype function:

Example :

```
<?
$ n = 10;
echo "Before is". gettype ($ n). "<br>";
settype ($ n, "string");
echo "After That is go". gettype ($ n);
?>
```

The isset function

To see if the variable is already created or not, it only requires the name of the variable you want to check for

Returns the value (1) if the variable is created and does not return any value if the variable is not created or exists.

Example :

```
<?
$ n = "n";
Echo isset ($ n);
?>
```

The function is unset

You delete the variable if it exists and free the memory from it (so make sure before you use this function to give a goodbye tear to the poor variable)

```
<?
$ n = "n";
unset ($ n);
Echo isset ($ n);
?>
```

The function is empty

Returns the value (1) if the variable is not generated or the value has zero (0) or empty text ("").

Time AND History

We can find the time and date by using PHP functions from these functions

gmdate ()

Example :

<?

Echo gmdate (m);

Echo gmdate (M);

?>

Note that there is a difference in the results although we use the same character, but the width varies when the character is large or small.

PHP holds many functions and reserved words that perform various operations such as complex calculations, finding the time and date, sending e-mails and stopping scripts for several seconds.These functions are not required for you to save them as you save your name, but you are required to understand what they do and use them at their convenience.

You can also view the day and month

Example

<?

Echo gmdate ("M D");

?>

Note that we used quotation marks to succeed when we used more than one operator in the function

Try the following code:

```
<?
Echo gmdate ("D, d M Y H H: i: s")
?>
```

Forms

Forms in the web or web pages are forms that you fill out and then when you send them to a web server (server) you receive a program that performs operations on them such as JavaScript, ASP or php (in our case).

Utility models

Say that you want to buy a book online, you actually need to fill out a form with your details, credit card number and other information.

In fact, you choose the book you want and write your name, phone number and mailbox (perhaps) in spaces or by referring to a range of options.

These values are stored in variables that are written in the name property (talked about in this lesson) and are sent when you press the submit button to the program that will process this data (which is specified in the ACTION property). Performing operations such as storing them in the database or sending them to e-mail through php.

What does the client do in forms?

In short, it fills textboxes, ticks the checkboxes, or sometimes votes for something, and selects a radio button.

These things are all created by the HTML and we studied for today to discuss how to create and how to deal and get data from them, we have to start to know that these tools actually arise between the two tags of the html language tags are tags

<form>

</form>

Characteristics of forms

The model combines all the characteristics of the host, but here we will look at two of them, ACTION and METHOD, which are widely used and important to us in our next lessons.

(ID; ClASS; NAME) need to deepen in HTML, especially when we enter into ACCEPT-CHAR and ENCTYPE and will be outside the scope of our subject at the moment and may be separated in future lessons, God willing.

ACTION

The function of this feature is to tell the server where the page is sending the form information or address of any kind, and of course in our case the second page will be the page that contains the php script.

It is not important that the page php may be html but it contains code to deal with an interactive program for web pages such as Java.

Let us give an example of this characteristic:


```
<FORM ACTION = "TEST.PHP">

... ..

</FORM>
```


METHOD

This feature tells the form how to send information to the target page. In fact, there are two known and well-known methods for sending information: GET and POST.

```
<FORM ACTION = "test.php" METHOD = "GET">
```

or

```
<FORM ACTIN = "test.php" METHOD = "POST">
```

Note / Actually there are more of these two ways to send the information they are

(CONNECT; HEAD; OPTIONS: DELETE: TRACE) and others, but only rarely.

Let us now separate these two methods further:

GET

This feature tells your web browser to add information written in the form to your web browser.

1- Write the title of the source page.

2 - followed by a question mark.

3- Writing titles and values.

http: //localhost/test.html? name = value

The last two points may not be well understood because you have never dealt with models before.

But the fact is that the form consists of elements (a check box, a text box, a radio button) and each of these elements has its own title (name) and each has its own value (value).

They are similar to variables and the page title can contain more than one name (name) and more than a value (value) and declare them using the (&) operator.

Example :

http: //localhost/test.html? animal = cat & age = 30

The extension that appears after the query String is called the result of the literal query.

The title is always in English (name) and we treat it as a variable name that should be defined on the target page (which we will write in PHP).

Values may contain spaces or parameters such as (+, -, \, #,%)

The browser uses URL ENCODING.

Also, URL ENCODING is used with Arabic or other non-English characters in character writing.

URL Encoding

There are some characters that the browser can not add to the title of the page in its true form, but uses the language of encryption in the definition of them and these tables of symbols, which uses the browser code instead of displaying in real

Do not worry, you do not have to save all these signs and encodings, but the browser will do the whole process for you.

POST

In fact, its function is the same as the get function, but it does not send information in the address of the web page, but rather put it in the body of the http response.

In addition, it can send data in a larger amount of GET.

Which is GET or POST?

The disadvantage of the GET feature may be the lack of confidentiality of the information you are typing and it can appear to the person sitting next to you ... especially when you want to keep your information confidential.

In addition, they are not useful in large text.

But it is useful in many things, for example search engines must use this feature so that the user can use the title of the search and keep it for another time and does not re-type the word that searches for.

POST is also useful in hiding information and containing large amounts of data, but you can not keep the title of the page .... However, it is also not so good in the protection that any hacker expert can get information if it does not have a certain encryption in the transfer .. But if you want To make it protected, you must use a protected connection to a protected server .... or what they call (SCURE CONNECTION TO SCURE SERVER).

Form controls:

In fact, the controls are regular text boxes (in which the user enters his or her name and address), radio buttons (in which the user chooses something (such as his favorite meal or drink)) and checkboxes (which allow the user to choose what he likes and likes from options). Displayed)

And also lists that help you choose more than one thing or one thing.

In most of these things the marking is used

<INPUT>

Its details are summarized as follows:

<INPUT TYPE = type NAME = name VALUE = value other attribute>

Explanation:

1 - TYPE = type

We determine the type of object if it is a radio button, a plain text box, or check boxes.

2 - NAME = name

You give the name of a variable in which the value is saved.

3 - VALUE = value

His job will become clearer when we include examples as his work differs from tool to tool.

Practical applications

In these applications we will create simple programs consisting of two files, the first file contains HTML code that creates the form and the second file receives and prints the results.

Text boxes (TEXT Box):

We do this as follows:

1 - Launch your text editor.

2 - Type the following code:

```
<html dir = "rtl">
```

```
<FORM METHOD = "GET" ACTION = "textbox.php">
```

What is your favorite meal in the morning?

```
<br>
<INPUT TYPE = "text" NAME = "food" value = "Cheese and jam">
<br>
<INPUT TYPE = submit VALUE = "Submit">
<INPUT TYPE = reset VALUE = "Clear">
</form>
</html>
```

3 - Save the file as an HTML page. Name it (textbox.html).

4 - Open the text editor if you close it.

5 - Type the following code:

```
<?
"Your favorite meal and to die in her love is". "". $ food;
?>
```

6 - Save the file as php. Name it textbox.php.

7 - Now take the two files and put them in your server folder.

8. Run the server and type in your Internet browser

http: //localhost/textbox.html

9 - Write your favorite meal and press the send button.

10. The result will appear.

Notice how the title appeared:

http: //localhost/textbox.php? food =% CC% C8% E4% C9 +% E6% E3% D1% C8% ED

Explanation

We initially created a page consisting of text, a text box, and a button that transmits data

We created the beginning of the form with the <FORM> tag and determined where the data will be sent by

 ACTION = "textbox.php"

We created the text box with the INPUT tag and selected the

 TYPE = "text"

We also set the default value in it by value

Value = "Cheese and jam"

We put the user-generated result in the text box in the food variable.

(Note that naming variables is case-sensitive in PHP and we haven't placed $ in the variable page in the html code).

And we've also added a button by

TYPE = SUBMIT

And we put a word on the button, the word (send)

VALUE = "Submit"

Also we made another button

Type = reset

And we made the phrase on it (cleared)

Value = "Clear"

There are two types of buttons: SUBMIT and RESET

1- The submit sends the information.

2. Reset erases data in all tools in the form for re-entry.

After we entered the data and pressed the submit button, the form sent the data to the page specified in the ACTION property and the selected page received the results in the form, which is one result in a text box whose value is saved in the food variable.

And printed with the echo function.

Since we used the GET method, we were given the title of the page in addition to (?) As well as the information recorded in the variables and where the URL ENCODING was used because it uses Arabic characters.

Large text boxes (larger text area).

If you want to write a multi-line message, you need a control that is quite different from the normal text box, which is the large text boxes where you can enter large and multi-line text.

This tool uses the Open tag and the Close tag

```
<TEXTAREA>
</TEXTAREA>
```

You can specify their size by specifying rows with columns and cols.

Practical exercise

1. Open your text editor

2- Type the following code:

```
<html dir = "rtl">
<FORM ACTION = "TAREA.PHP" METHOD = "POST">
what is your favourite meal ?
<br>
<TEXTAREA NAME = "food" ROWS = "10" COLS = "50">
cheese
jam
Pasta
Beef Burger
Samosa
Blindfolded
Applied
Machadona
Sincerely, if I sit down type haha
</TEXTAREA>
```

```
<br>

<INPUT TYPE = SUBMIT VALUE = "Send requests to the barkeeper">

</FORM>

</html>
```

3. Save the file as TAREA.html.

4. Now open a new file in the text editor.

5- Write the following code:

```
<html dir = "rtl">

Your favorite meal is:

<br>

<?

Echo $ food;

?>

</html>
```

6. Save the file as tarea.php

7. Put them in your server folder.

8. Run the program.

http: //localhost/tarea.html

9. Press the button to send the data.

10 - See the result.

Explanation

Adding something to say here, except that we want you to notice how we prepared the default value by writing texts between the tags of textarea and also that we used the method POST in sending data, which made it does not appear in the address bar.

NAME specifies the variable name to which the value will go and the variable name in the code does not contain $ because it is HTML code and not PHP.

More than one option at a time!

In fact, we may see checkboxes on web pages when we want to sign up for a particular site to see its contents or when we want to register an email or reserve space at a site.

Its usefulness is to provide an opportunity for the user to determine the types of things he wants to participate in, for example, an opportunity to accept an agreement or otherwise, reject everyone or accept everyone.

We can manufacture the tag box by tag INPUT

<INPUT TYPE = "CHECKBOX" NAME = "swalif" value = "Sideburns" checked>

We define the tool type as a check box in this pane

TYPE = "CHECKBOX"

We specify the variable name in this pane

NAME = "swalif"

We specify the value that is placed in the variable if the user selects the check box in this pane:

value = "Sideburns"

If you do not set the value option, the default value is on when the user selects the check box and it is blank if the user does not check the box.

We set the default value by adding the word checked. If this word is placed, the check box is automatically selected. If we do not, it will be checked.

Checked

Practical Application (1):

1- Open Notepad and write the following code:

```
<html dir = "rtl">
<FORM ACTION = "CHECK.PHP" METHOD = "POST">
What do you want to do in life? (You can choose more than one answer)
<br>
<INPUT TYPE = "CHECKBOX" NAME = "WIFE" CHECKED>
What I want to do in life is to get married and be saved from death.
<br>
<input type = submit value = "Submit">
</FORM>
```

</html>

2. Save the file as check.html.

3- Open a new file in Notepad and write the following:

```
<?
Echo $ WIFE;
?>
```

4. Save the file as check.php.

5. Move the two files to the server folder.

6. Type in your browser

http: //localhost/check.html

7. The result

Practical Application (2):

1. Open Notepad and type the following code and save it in a new file named check2.html

```
<html dir = "rtl">
<FORM ACTION = "CHECK2.PHP" METHOD = "POST">
What do you want to do in life? (You can choose more than one answer)
<br>
<INPUT TYPE = "CHECKBOX" NAME = "WIFE" value = "Wife" CHECKED>
```

What I want to do in life is to get married and be saved from death.

<INPUT TYPE = "CHECKBOX" NAME = "jihad" value = "Jihad">

I want the souls of jihad and shed the heads of infidels and polytheists

<INPUT TYPE = "CHECKBOX" NAME = "qran" value = "QURAN" CHECKED>

 By God, if I join the memorization of the Koran and memorize the whole Koran and apply it in my work and my life Hrtah in my life many

<input type = submit value = "Submit">

</FORM>

</html>

2- Open a new file and place the following code in it:

<html dir = "rtl">

<?

Echo $ WIFE. "". $ jihad. "". $ qran;

?>

</html>

3- Save it as check2.php

4. Run the file.

5. The result

Practical application (3)

1- Open the text editor and type the following code:

```
<html dir = "rtl">

<FORM ACTION = "CHECK3.PHP" METHOD = "POST">

What do you want to do in life? (You can choose more than one answer)

<br>

<INPUT TYPE = "CHECKBOX" NAME = "alswalif []" value = "Wife" CHECKED>

What I want to do in life is to get married and be saved from death.

<br>

<INPUT TYPE = "CHECKBOX" NAME = "alswalif []" value = "Flag">

I want to become a scientist

<br>

<INPUT TYPE = "CHECKBOX" NAME = "alswalif []" value = "Money" CHECKED>

I want to become a Mayonera

<br>

<input type = submit value = "Submit">

</FORM>

</html>
```

2- Save it as check3.html and open the text editor again and type the following code:

```
<html dir = "rtl">

<?

Echo "$ alswalif [0] <br>";
```

Echo "$ alswalif [1]
";

Echo "$ alswalif [2]
";

?>

</html>

3- Save it as check3.php and transfer it to the server file.

4. Run the program

http: //localhost/check.html

5 - Click the send button and see the result

Explanation

In fact, we have applied three exercises. We wanted to point out that we did not use the value for the variable and the value was given on when the user selected the tag box. For more than one check box, we have added values that are placed in the variables when the user selects them, as in the second exercise. Matrices now but we wanted to draw your eyes only, and we will speak about matrices in detail in the lessons coming, God willing, it is Duplicates After talking about conditional statements in the PHP.

Radio buttons (RADIO BUTTONS) (Choose your favorite drink!)

What is your favorite choice? Note that you can not choose more than one option !!

In fact, the radio button allows you to choose one of several options and see it a lot at the program agreements where it gives you the opportunity to either accept or reject the agreement and be one of the two options selected (the option of rejection!).

The radio buttons are used using the <INPUT> statement as follows:

<INPUT TYPE = "radio" NAME = "name" value = "value" checked>

We define the object type as a radio button in this pane:

TYPE = "radio"

We define the variable name in this part:

NAME = "name"

We specify the value that will be in the variable here:

value = "value"

In fact, with the radio azar we make the name variable the same and the values are different

For each question. If we do not set a value, PHP will set the value on to the variable.

practical application :

1. Run your text editor and type the following code and save it in a file named radio.html.

<html dir = "rtl">

<form action = radio.php method = "post">

what is your favorite drink ?


```
<br>

<INPUT TYPE = "radio" NAME = "mshroob" value = "Tea" checked>

Tea

<br>

<INPUT TYPE = "radio" NAME = "mshroob" value = "Coffee">

coffee

<br>

<INPUT TYPE = submit value = "Submit">


</form>

</html>
```

2. Open the text editor and type the following code and save it as radio.php

```
<html dir = "rtl">

<?

"Your favorite drink is:". "". $ mshroob;

?>

</html>
```

3 - Select your favorite drink and choose Send.

Explanation:

In fact we have created radio buttons and we have set a value for each button that belongs to the phrase next to the button. We have checked to see how the tool containing the statement is automatically selected and notice that the statement next to the button is located below the button code such as:

<INPUT TYPE = "radio" NAME = "mshroob" value = "Tea" checked>

Tea

The phrase is colored in red.

Also note that we used only one variable for all the choices so that all the buttons whose value goes back to that variable.

Lists Or drop down menus Choose your wife's future specifications and name:

The menus in html are used slightly differently from the previous tools, since we use two tags from the html tags:

<select> Let's create the list and <OPTION> and use the MULTIPLE property if we want to allow the user to choose more than one value and put the value chosen by the user in a variable by the property NAME or in the array of variables (and the concept of your arrays well in the lesson of matrices, God willing .

practical application :

1.Open your text editor and type the following code and save it in a file named lists.html:

```html
<html dir = "rtl">
<form action = "lists.php" method = "post">
What do you want to be the name of the future wife (unmarried)?
<br>
<select name = "wife">
<option> Hana </option>
<option> Jumana </option>
<option> Razan </option>
<option> Magic </option>
<option> Sarah </option>
<option> toxicity </option>
<option> Rowan </option>
<option> Dalal </option>
<option> Other name </option>
</select>
<br>
What do you want their specifications to be?
<Br>
<select name = "dis []" multiple>
<option> Beautiful </option>
<option> Religious </option>
<option> Blonde </option>
<option> Hairless people </option>
```

```
<option> Black </option>

<option> Brown </option>

<option> White </option>

</select>

<br>

<INPUT TYPE = SUBMIT VALUE = "Send">

</html>
```

2- Open a new file and type the following code and save it as lists.php:

```
<html dir = "rtl">

<?

Echo "I wanted to be your wife's name". "". $ wife;

Echo "<br> <br>";

Echo "I wanted to be their specification";


Echo "<br> <br>";

Echo "$ dis [0] <br>";

Echo "$ dis [1] <br>";

Echo "$ dis [2] <br>";

Echo "$ dis [3] <br>";

Echo "$ dis [4] <br>";

Echo "$ dis [5] <br>";

Echo "$ dis [6] <br>";
```

```
?>
```

```
</html>
```

Run the program

http: //localhost/lists.html

Select what you want and click the Submit button

Explanation:

We have created a list that allows the selection of one value of them and then this value goes to the variable wife and we made a second list that allows the selection of more than one element and we put these values in the array of variables (the meaning of the matrices will be clear in the next lessons, God willing).

Hidden tool (and secret information!)

There are times when you need to send some information from a web page to another web page via forms and at the same time you don't want the user to see this information.

In fact, there is a tool that helps you hide this information from the user called the hidden form field or hidden tool (hidden form field or hidden control).

This tool plays a different role and distinct from the rest of the tools is to hide the information entered as we explained in the past and is very useful with models made by PHP as it also allows us to be hidden information are variables PHP.

These hidden fields are made as follows:

<INPUT TYPE = HIDDEN NAME = hidden1 VALUE = "Secret Message">

We place HIDDEN so that the browser knows that this information is hidden (does not appear to the user) and we name the variable that holds the information, which stores its name in the NAME and put the information we want to hide in the VALUE.

We can also benefit from it by php by typing the HTML code with the command echo () in PHP as in the following example:

```
<?
$ msg1 = "This statement will not appear";
Echo "<form>";
Echo "<input type = hidden name = secret value =' $ msg1 '>";
Echo "<input type = submit>";
Echo "</form>";
?>
```

This code you see is HTML code written in PHP by the command echo () and we were able to store the value of the php variable ($ msg) in the html (secret) variable.

practical application :

1 - Open the text editor and type the following code and save it as hid.php:

```
<html dir = "rtl">
<head> </head>
<body>
<?
$ car1 = "Lexus";
$ car2 = "Maxima";
$ car3 = "Land Cruiser";
Echo "<form method = get action =' hid2.php '>";
Echo "What car would you like to buy or have?";
Echo "
<select name = 'favcar'>
<option> $ car1 </option>
<option> $ car2 </option>
<option> $ car3 </option>
</select> <br> <br>
<input type = hidden name = hid1 value = '$ car1'>
<input type = hidden name = hid2 value = '$ car2'>
<input type = hidden name = hid3 value = '$ car3'>
<input type = submit value = 'Submit'>
</form> ";
```

```
?>

</body>

</html>
```

3- Open the text editor and type the following code and save it as hid2.php

```
<html dir = "rtl">

<head> </head>

<body>

<?

Echo "We have shown you the following cars: <br>";

Echo "$ hid1 <br>";

Echo "$ hid2 <br>";

Echo "$ hid3 <br>";

Echo "<br> You have chosen: <br>";

Echo $ favcar;

?>

</body>

</html>
```

3 - I moved the two files to the server folder and then run the script:

http: //localhost/hid.php

Explanation:

We have created a php script. Note that we used the '') instead of (") as we were working in the html, because we said earlier that the literal values .... (see variables lesson) and we have included the values of php variables in Html code which saves us a lot of rewriting (in case the text is long).

Read the example more than once and you will become clear more article, God willing.

Using password fields

In order to make the information more secure from being stolen or otherwise you can use the password fields which is a simple text box that shows text in the form of stars **** If the device is used by more than one person, this method is a little good in That someone does not show the other's confidential information.

In fact, however, you will not be protected if the method used to send user data is the get method unless you use data encryption and it is more good if you use the post method and also will not be protected from the hacker if you do not use SSL (Secure Socket Layer) in order to Activates data encryption.

practical application

Open your text editor and type the following code and save it as pass.php

```
<html dir = "rtl">

<body>

<form method = post action = "pass1.php">

user name

<br>

<input type = "text" name = "user">
```

```
<br>

password

<input type = "password" name = "pass">

<br>

<input type = submit value = 'Submit'>

</form>

<body>

</html>
```

Open your text editor and type the following code and save it as pass1.php

```
<?

"The username is:";

Echo "<br> $ user <br>";

"The password is:";

Echo "<br> <br> $ pass"

<?
```

Move the two files to your server folder

Run the program and note the result.

Send email by php:

E-mail is the life that beats scripts. For example, there are scripts send mail to the owner of the site to tell him something or a note or other and can be used in more than one area.

The function used in this is the mail () function

mail ("$ to", "$ sub", "$ msg", "From: $ you");

You place the mail that the message will receive in the $ to cell, the subject of the message in the $ sub cell, the message in the $ msg field, your mail or the sender's mail in the $ you field.

practical application

Type the following code and save it in a file named mail.html

```
<html dir = rtl>
<head>
   <title> Mail sending program </title>
</head>
<body>
<form action = "mail.php" method = "post">
sender's address
<br>
```

```
<input type = "text" name = "you">

<br>

Future address

<br>

<input type = "text" name = "to">

<br>

Message Subject

<input type = "text" name = "sub">

<br>

the message

<textarea rows = 10 cols = 20 name = "msg">

</textarea>

<input type = "submit" value = "send email">

</form>

</body>

</html>
```

Create another file, type the following code and give it the name mail.php.

```
<?

mail ("$ to", "$ sub", "$ msg", "From: $ you");

?>
```

Put the two files in the server folder and run the program and fill in the data and press the send button and you will see that the message was sent successfully.

Practical programs

The program or script sending cards is simple

It contains two files, one with tags and an e-mail address, and the other with the transmission

The first file is chcard.php and its code is as follows:

```
<html dir = "rtl">

<form action = card.php method = "post">

Select the card you want to send

<br>

<br>
```

```
<INPUT TYPE = "radio" NAME = "card" value =
"http://www.khalaad.f2s.com/MADINA9_small.JPG" checked>
```

The first card

```
<br>
```

```
<br>
```

```
<img src = "http://www.khalaad.f2s.com/MADINA9_small.JPG" width =
"100" height = "100" alt = "" border = 0>
```

```
<br>
```

```
<br>
```

```
<INPUT TYPE = "radio" NAME = "card" value =
"http://www.khalaad.f2s.com/Haram3.jpg">
```

The second card

```
<br>
```

```
<img src = "http://www.khalaad.f2s.com/Haram3.jpg" width = "100" height
= "100" alt = "" border = 0>
```

```
<br>
```

Your Name

```
<br>
```

```
<input type = "text" name = "myname">
```

```
<br>
```

Your E-mail

```
<br>
```

```
<input type = "text" name = "you">
```

```
<br>
```

Your friend's e-mail


```html
<input type = "text" name = "to">
```


Congratulation theme

```html
<input type = "text" name = "sub">
```


the message


```html
<textarea rows = 10 cols = 20 name = "msg">
</textarea>
```



```html
<INPUT TYPE = submit value = "Send Card">
</form>
</html>
```

The second file will send the card and write the following code and save it in a file named card.php

```php
<?
$ message = "$ myname has sent you a card". "\ N". "He says in the text of his letter to you: \ n $ msg". "You can find it on the following link." "\ N". "$ Card". "\ N";

mail ("$ to", "$ sub", "$ message", "From: $ you");
```

```
echo "<center> Your message has been sent successfully </center>";

?>
```

Note :

The \ n function just starts a new line because we cannot use <br> in the body of the message

Conditional commands

We have taken in the previous lessons an idea of the variables and how to deal with data models ... In this lesson we will learn how to control the code in the sense of implementing a certain line of code when a certain condition and when it does not ignore the line and go to the next line .. This gives us greater control of the code It makes us use excellent decisions and implement great things and PHP programs.

Let's give you an idea of our daily life ....

You get up in the morning and want to prepare your breakfast which consists of the following:

honey

cheese

bread

Tea

You will go to the refrigerator and then look for things that make up your breakfast.If you do not find what you want to go to the mall to buy your need, go to the kitchen and make sure again and look for the supplies that the house needs in general.

1. Look for cheese and if you do not find it go to step 3.

2 - If you find cheese you are looking for honey if you find it move to step 4, and if you do not find it move to step 5.

3 - you write them in a side sheet and look for honey.

4 - prepare to go to the mall.

5 - write it in a side paper and then prepare to go to the mall.

Did you notice that you were searching for certain things, if you find (true) you search for the next and if you do not find it (false) you recorded in your shopping list.

Boolean values and conditional functions

In fact, we talked about the variables before and we mentioned that there are logical variables (their value is either true or false) and we did not explain them, and this lesson will explain them and give examples of how to deal with them.

The IF statement

IF condition is true (if true)

{

excute this code (execute this code)

}

The IF function is known in almost all programming languages ... it performs a verification of a certain object and performs some things if the condition is true (true) and doing other things if it is not true ....

PHP will only implement code between {and} if the condition is true.

If not, he will override it and execute the code that follows.

You can also make it with one line and don't use parentheses.

IF condition is true excute function;

Note that you must use {and} if the code is multiple lines, but if it is one line, you don't need to use it.

The following two examples are all true

Example 1

<?

$ S = 10

IF ($ S = 10) echo 11;

?>

Example 2

<?

$ S = 10

```
IF ($ S = 10) {

 echo 11;

}

?>
```

Imagine, for example, that it is rainy and we will give the rain variable and we call rain and give the umbrella the name of another variable and we call umbrella and we will assume that there is a command in php called go out Ok now the code we want to write is:

```
If $ rain = true

{

$ umberrlla = true

}
go out ();
```

The usefulness of this code is to order PHP to carry the umbrella ($ umberrlla = true) with it if it is raining ($ rain = true) and if it is not raining and the condition is not met then it will go out to the picnic without any umbrella.

Of course there is no function to do this, but we did so in order to clarify the user structure of the function in general.

Introduction to Boolean Values

Boolean values symbolize things that are intolerable to more than two possibilities, which are either true or false, a new kind of value other than what we previously knew (such as numeric and textual).

Example

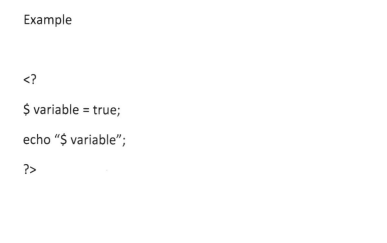

```
<?

$ variable = true;

echo "$ variable";

?>
```

If you see the result you will find that it prints the number one, the value of the variable if it is true, but if it is wrong or incorrect, its value will be (0).

Boolean transactions

We have already taken mathematical coefficients in some detail (+, -, /, *) and now we will take something new from the coefficients, which are logical coefficients that help us in making conditions and restrictions on something and give us more control over the code.

Transactions: <and>

You are supposed to be familiar with both the greater than and the smallest marks in the math you learn in school, which makes understanding this optimization simple.

```
<?

If (6> 5)

{

echo "number six is greater than number five";

}

Echo "end";

?>
```

In our example, PHP will check the condition (6> 5). If it is true, it will print the line (the number six is greater than the number five) and then print the end. If not, it will ignore the code and print only (end).

We can also use it to compare variable and number or between variable and constant or vice versa or compare two variables.

Example 1

```
<html dir = "rtl">
```

```
<?

$ LuckeyNumber = 5;

If ($ LuckeyNumber <6)

{

echo ("lucky number is smaller than number six");

}

?>
```

Example 2

```
<html dir = "rtl">

<?

$ f = 5;

$ r = 10;

If ($ f> $ r)

{

echo "$ f is greater than $ r";

}

?>
```

practical application :

Launch the text editor, type the following code and save it as thegame.php

```
<html dir = "rtl">
<body>
<form method = get action = "game.php">
What is the number I am thinking now which is between 1 and 10?
<input type = "text" name = "number">
<br>
<br>
<input type = submit>
</form>
</body>
</html>
```

Open your text editor again and type the following code and save it as game.php

```
<html dir = "rtl">
<body>
<?
$ num = rand (1,10);
if ($ number> $ num)
{
```

```
echo "I chose a larger number than I think";

Echo "The number I think of is";

Echo $ num;

Echo "<br>". "We really regret that you did not succeed, we hope to tell
you in the coming times";

}
if ($ number <$ num)

{

echo "I chose a smaller number than I think";

Echo "The number that was in my mind is $ num";

Echo "<br>". "We really regret that you did not succeed, we hope to tell
you in the coming times";

}
?>
you passed
</body>
</html>
```

Application Explanation:

Rand function

This function selects a random number from two digits to which the first
number (x) is the smallest and the second is the largest (y)

Rand (x, y);

You can directly save the value that this function outputs in a variable

Example

$ Num = rand (5.57);

This shows what we have done in the code

$ num = rand (1,10);

We have chosen a random value and then compared it with the value entered by the user if the value entered by the user is greater than the value of the random number told us that the number you enter is greater than the correct number ... This is evident in the following lines:

```
if ($ number> $ num)
{
echo "I chose a larger number than I think";
Echo "The number I think of is";
Echo $ num;
Echo "<br>". "We really regret that you did not succeed, we hope to tell you in the coming times";
}
```

If the condition does not apply and the number chosen by the user is smaller than the random number, it leaves the first condition and goes to the second condition and applies the commands in which it tells him that the number he chose is smaller than the required number, and this is evident in the following lines:

if ($ number <$ num)

{

echo "I chose a smaller number than I think";

Echo "The number that was in my mind is $ num";

Echo "<br>". "We really regret that you did not succeed, we hope to tell you in the coming times";

}

If the two conditions do not apply, he leaves them and writes the word (I succeeded) without any other words as we were writing the word (we regret that you did not succeed, we hope to tell you in the next times) before the word (I succeeded), I hope you have understood well what I say. ... and this statement is evident in the following lines:

?>

you passed

</body>

</html>

Thus, we have created a complete game that tells the user when he succeeds or loses.

Equality coefficients: == and ===

Previously we used the individual equal sign to store a value in a variable and we take a kind of equal sign: double equal sign (==) and double equal sign (===).

We used the individual or regular equal sign to store values in variables.

Example :

```
<?
$ m = 12;
?>
```

But the signs we are talking about are used to determine if one value is equal to another.

Example :

```
<?
$ m = "11";
$ u = 11;
If ($ m == $ u)
{
Echo "Equal values";
}
?>
```

Note that $ m is a literal variable and $ u is a numeric variable.

If we want to return a value to a variable, we use the normal equal sign (=) and if we want to test two variables or a certain value of being equal, we test the values with the double equal sign (==).

In php4.01, a new equal sign is issued that tests the values and gives the value (true) only if the value types are equal and the data types in the variables are also equal.

Example 1:

```
<?
$ m = "11";
$ u = 11;
If ($ m == $ u)
{
Echo "Equal values";
}
?>
```

Example 2:

```
<?
$ m = "11";
$ u = 11;
If ($ m === $ u)
{
Echo "Equal values";
}
?>
```

Illustration

Note that in the first example we used the double equal sign to test the values and the values were equal in the two variables so the values were printed equal (although the data type is different) but in the second example when we used the double equal sign nothing is printed because the values are equal but the data type is different The variable $ m is literal while the variable $ u is numeric.

Transactions: =! And <>

The opposite of the sign of equality is the sign of inequality (! =)

Example :

```
<?
If (5! = 99) echo "Values are not equal";
?>
```

Note that 5 is not equal to 99, so the condition is true, so it prints that the values are not equal.

The opposite of a sign greater than and less than the <> sign, returns a value of true if the two values are different from each other, ie it is almost like a! = Sign.

Example :

```
<?
If (5 <> 99) echo "Values are not equal";
?>
```

Practical application of signs of equality and inequality

Open your text editor and type the following code:

```html
<html>
<head> </head>
<body>
<Form method = get ACTION = "quiz.php">
What is the name of the man called Farouk?
<br> <br>
<input type = "radio" name = "man" value = "age">
Omar bin al-Khattab may Allah be pleased with him
<br>
<input type = "radio" name = "man" value = "أبوبكر">
Abu Bakr, may Allah be pleased with him
<br>
<input type = "radio" name = "man" value = "osman">
Othman bin Affan may Allah be pleased with him
<br>
<input type = submit>
</form>
</body>
```

</html>

Save it as quiz.html ...

Open your text editor and type the following code:

```
<html dir = "rtl">

<head> </head>

<body>

<?

If ($ q == "age") echo "The answer is correct";

If ($ q! = "عمر") echo "The answer is wrong";

?>
```

Save it as quiz.php and place it in the server folder

Run the quiz.html file

Boolean operators (AND, OR, NOT)

These logical operators allow you to execute the code after checking a set of conditions and also execute the code if more than one condition is met: (AND)

Or check something out of several things: (OR)

For example, you can verify that something is incorrect in order to do something else: (NOT)

For example, you can say: If it is rainy and the storm is too strong, I will not go out.

You can say: If the weather is calm or there is no rain, I will go out to the park.

You can also say: If it is not rainy I will go for a walk.

However, when using these functions, you must keep these conditions in parentheses.

Modulus (AND) and its counterpart (&&)

We can use the AND and && arguments to validate several conditions for the execution of a given object

Example 1

```
<?
$ w = 10;
$ g = 12;
IF ($ w = 10 and $ g = 12) echo ("All conditions met");
?>
```


Example 2

```
<?
```

```
$ w = 10;

$ g = 12;

IF ($ w = 10 && $ g = 15) echo ("All conditions met");

?>
```

In the previous two examples, we have verified more than one condition using the (&& and and) parameters. When all conditions were met, the order was executed.

Note that we have set the conditions in parentheses () for the code to work properly:

```
($ w = 10 && $ g = 15)

($ w = 10 and $ g = 12)
```

Modulus (OR) and its counterpart (||)

The OR operator verifies several conditions and if any one of them is executed, it executes the code and its counterpart (||) which performs the same operation.

Example 1

```
<?

$ E = 100;

$ T = 8;

IF ($ E = 14 OR $ E = 55 OR $ E = 10 OR $ T = 8) echo ("One of these conditions has been met");

?>
```

Example 2

```
<?
$ E = 100;
$ T = 458;
IF ($ E = 14 || $ E = 55 || $ E = 10 || $ T = 8) echo ("One of these conditions
has been met");
?>
```

So when one of these conditions is met, the line is printed (one of these conditions has been met).

Note It may not be that important, but you should know that the symbols && and || It has precedence and priority over the use of AND and OR.

OPERATION NOT AND HIS (!)

In fact, you can never use NOT because it is not already present in PHP, but you can use the parameter (!) As an alternative. It performs the same function of making sure that there is an incorrect value (FALSE) in order to do something.

```
<?
$ F = "Knight";
IF! ($ F == "Noman") echo ("Welcome");
?>
```

In the previous example, PHP makes sure that the variable $ F does not contain the literal value (Noman). This is done using the parameter (!) And when it is checked it prints the line (Welcome)

Note that when we test a variable with a parameter (!), PHP if the variable is empty or not created gives it a value of zero, FALSE.

Example

IF (! ($ R)) echo (10);

Use transactions <= and> =

A well-known and well-known coefficients in mathematics are the signs less than or equal to <= or greater than or equal to =.

```
<?
$ t = 15;
If ($ t> = 10) echo ("Excellent". "<br>");
$ t = 5;
If ($ t <= 9) echo ("very good");
?>
```

Aggregate transactions

In a condition, we can check a set of values using a set of coefficients, and aggregate these groups into parentheses () as we previously used more than one (+, -, /, *) with parentheses.

This will be evident in our example:

```
<?
$ a = 10;
$ y = 5;
$ t = 29;
If (($ a == 10) or ($ a == 54) and ($ y! = 25) and ($ t> = 11)) echo "all conditions are met";
?>
```

18 will be printed because the value of the previous expression grouping is correct. If we explain the example, we will see the first section:

($ a == 10) or ($ a == 54)

Of course, the variable has a value of 10, so this portion will be true.

Then we see the part:

($ y! = 25) and ($ t> = 11)

Of course all the conditions were checked and the word was printed (all the conditions were met).

Multiple conditions (else if and else)

For example, we can use more than one syntax:

If condtion is true

{

Excute code

}

Else

{

Excute other code

}

It checks the condition. If it finds it, it executes the first code and if it does not, it will execute the other code.

Example

```
<?

$ age = 10;

If ($ age> 18)

{

echo "Welcome to the largest e - commerce site";

}

else

{
```

echo "Children are not allowed to enter the site because they do not have money";

}

?>

We can also use the following structure:

If condtion is true

{

Excute code

}

Elseif

{

Excute other code

}

Else

{

Excute other code

}

It applies more than one condition. If none of the conditions is true, the code after the word else will be executed. Example :

```
<?
$ age = 10;
If ($ age <= 18)
{
echo "Welcome to the largest e - commerce site";
```

```
}
elseif ($ y> = 44);
{
echo "No problem if you are big";
}
else
{
echo "Rest is forbidden";
}
?>
```

Nesting conditional phrases

You can nest conditional statements, and we mean nesting conditional phrases is to nest the conditions, for example, if one condition is true, it must be another condition is true in order for something to happen and so on.

Example :

```
<?
$ h = "ahmed";
$ f = 45;
If ($ h = = "ahmed")
{If ($ f = = 45)
{
echo "The name and number are correct";
```

```
}
else
{
echo ("Invalid number");
}}
else {
echo "Invalid login name";
}
?>
```

This is just a very simple example of nesting conditional functions where it performs a test on a certain value and then passes that test successfully it performs a second test. If the second test is passed, the name and number are printed correctly.

practical application

In this application we will create a simple contest in which we use what we talked about previously

1. Create a Msabqa.html file.

2- Write the following code in it:

```
<html>
<body>


<form method = "POST" action = "msabqa.php" dir = "rtl">
Who is the first adult caliph
```

```html
<p> <br> <input type = "radio" value = "abubaker" name = "s"> أبوبكر الصديق
<br> <input type = "radio" value = "3mar" name = "s"> عمر

<br> <input type = "radio" value = "3thman" checked name = "s"> Osman
<br> <br> <br>


</p>


 <p> <input type = "submit" value = "submit"> <input type = "reset" value =
"delete"> </p>
</form>


</body> <html>
```

Open a file and name it msabqa.php

```php
<?
<html dir = "rtl">
If $ s == "3mar" {
The answer is correct
}
else
{
echo "Wrong answer";
}
?>
```

The Switch statement

```
Switch (VARIABLE) {
CASE THING1:
Excute code;
        break;
CASE THING2:
Excute code;
break;
 Default;
Excute code;


 }
```

The statement does the same as the if statement, but with a more intuitive and granular structure and lets you test the value of a variable and do more than test it.

 break;

You exit a specific statement such as switch and if and go to the commands and phrases after.

 EXIT;

The process of exit from the code is final and do not apply any commands after, and in the following illustrative example you will find that break; Exit only the statement while the exit; You exit the entire code.

Example :

```
<?
$ s = 10;
if ($ s = 10) {
echo "number = 10";
exit;
}
elseif ($ s <11) {
  echo "number is less than 11"
{
echo "hello";
?>
```


Example :

```
<?
$ s = 10;
if ($ s = 10) {
echo "number = 10";
break;
}
```

```
elseif ($ s <11) {

  echo "number is less than 11"

{

echo "Hello";

?>
```

Defualt;

If all cases in the Switch statement are not correct, the commands that are after this word will be executed and do almost the same as else in the if statement.

Example 1
```
<?
$ g = "ahmed";
Switch ($ g) {
Case "ahmed":
Echo "Allowed";
Break;
  Case "khaled":
Echo "Forbidden";
```

```php
Break;
  Case "salem":
Echo "Forbidden";
Break;
  Case "Mohmed":
Echo "Allowed";
Break;
Default;
Echo "You have entered an invalid name";
}
?>
```

Example 2

```php
Switch ($ g) {
Case $ g> 50:
"Great";
Break;
  Case 40:
Echo "La Pace";
Break;
  Case ($ g <15):
Echo "Children forbidden";
Break;
```

Case 30:

Echo "Allowed";

Break;

}

Note that when we test texts we need double quotation marks and when the numbers we don't need that.

practical application

Open your text editor and type the following code and save it as age.html

```
<html>
<form method = post action = "age.php">
```

how old are you ?

<input type = "text" name = "g">

<input type = submit value = "Submit">

</form>

</html>

Open your text editor and type the following code and save it as age.php

```
<?
Switch ($ g) {
Case $ g> 50:
"Great";
Break;
  Case 40:
Echo "La Pace";
Break;
  Case ($ g <15):
Echo "Children forbidden";
Break;
  Case 30:
Echo "Allowed";
Break;
}
```

?>

Explanation

The Switch statement tests the value of a variable and you can do more than assume it and you must type the word break; In order to stop the execution of the switch statement, for example, if you type the following code:

```
<?
$ g = 40
Switch ($ g) {
Case $ g <50:
Echo "1";

 Case 40:
Echo "2";
}
?>
```

If the user enters the number 40 will be printed numbers one and two both because you did not stop the phrase completed the verification and applied all required operations.

Get rid of the html tags

If you put a text box and want the user to type something in it, it can enter anything and suppose it was written in the text box as follows:

I am <b> ahmed </b>...

The browser will display it after processing as follows:

I am ahmed....

Let us do a practical application

Open the text editor and type the following code and save it as htmlch.html

```
<html dir = "rtl">

<form method = post action = "html.php">

Enter your name

<br>

<input type = "text" name = "fname">

<input type = submit value = "Submit">

</form>

</html>
```

Open the text editor and type the following code and save it as html.php

```
<?

"This is the natural form of the phrase when printed";

Echo "<br>". $ fname;

?>
```

Put the files in the server folder and then run the file htmlch.html and type in the text box anything placed between the tags and html

Example :

I am <a>alfareees </i>

You will find that the tags are treated as html and not as plain text. To display them as plain text, you use the function

HtmlSpecialChars ();

It will treat the html code as just plain and natural text.

So we modify the html.php file to read as follows:

```
<?
$ fname = HtmlSpecialChars ($ fname);
"This is the shape after using the function";
Echo "<br>". $ fname;
 ?>
```

Duplicates and arrays

In the previous lesson we took some of the basics of programming, which are conditional functions and decision-making and now we are heading to something that loves the computer work is duplicates and matrices.

In fact, you may have something to do daily, such as breakfast early in the morning and sleep in the evening, you continue to this routine always .... We call this thing in programming language repetition.

There is something else called matrices ... In fact, your office drawer may contain several drawers, the first drawer contains Islamic books and the second drawer contains sports books and the third drawer contains math books ... Or suppose you are a teacher in a school and you have Table of classes in the first class you have for example teaching mathematics .... and the second class you have teaching science and the third you have teaching chemistry .... Your classes arranged in a certain way, although they are all called classes, but each session is different from the other in the article! It is ranked in ascending order (1st, 2nd, 3rd .....).

We call this technique matrices .... Matrices is a variable named fixed and have more than one value and each value has a certain number and in order to get the value you write the variable and then the value of the value, which does not require that these values are sequential there may be two values and each value of a number is different The distance from the second value is exemplified by example 1 and 258, which are completely different and are far from the other.

Combining duplicates with arrays helps you save the number of lines of code and helps you create fantastic things in as few lines as possible.

Duplicates

Iterations are a repetition of a certain order a certain number of times and we have previously taken conditional functions or conditional statements more correctly and we found that the code that we write in the conditional statements are implemented only when the condition is true

Also iterates it tests the condition if its value is correct it does the required code and then re-test the value if it is true it re-execute the code and so on, but when the condition is not true it stops executing the code and the program is completed normally ... There are three Types of duplicates.

The first function we take at the beginning is the while function

Repetition while

We have taken the iteration while because it is very simple and its formula is:

While (condition)

{

code

}

Example :

```
<?
$ d = 10;
while ($ d <15)
{
echo "$ d <br>";
$ d ++;
}
```

?>

PHP will first give the variable $ d the value 10 and then start the iteration while if the condition is true (that is, the variable is smaller than the number 15) it executes the code in parentheses and this code prints the variable and then adds one to the value in The variable $ d and then the condition will be tested again and if it is true, the same process will be done until the condition is incorrect and then stop iteration and complete the code after the parentheses.

If you do not end the repetition, the repetition will not stop and may be infinite ....

Example :

```
<?
$ d = 10;
while ($ d <15)
{
echo "$ d <br>";
}
?>
```

The number 10 will be printed and the repetition will not stop because the condition is always true and there is nothing to stop it. In the previous code we were able to stop the code because we added one to the value in the variable. From 15.

Repeat do - while

This iteration works in the same way as the first iteration, but there are some minor differences and its formula is as follows:

do

code

while (condition condition);

Example :

```
<?
$ f = 15;
do
{
echo "$ f";
$ f ++
}
while ();
```

The iteration will execute the line between the parentheses first and then perform the condition test. If the condition is true, it will repeat the operation between the parentheses, which is one addition to the variable $ f. Any work while in the second iteration we implemented the code first and then we performed the test.

Repetition FOR

This repetition differs from its predecessors but its function is the same as their function is to repeat commands when something happens

Formula:

For (counter counter; test value; set counter Perform an operation on the counter)

{

code

}

Example :

<?

For ($ u = 18; $ u> 10; $ u--)

{

echo $ u;

}

?>

This iteration consists of three sections .... The first section we put a variable containing a value where the iteration will start from this value and the second section we write the condition that the iteration will examine (which is as usual test for the value of the variable in the first section) and the third section we put The work that will be done on the variable at each iteration and then we write the code that will perform the iteration between the parentheses.

As if we tell the php in general to initially give the variable $ u value 18 and before it executes the code it has to analyze the condition. If the condition is true, it decreases one of the variable $ u and the code is executed until the variable $ u becomes 9 and the PHP then Exit the repetition and go to the code that follows the parentheses.

Arrays

We have already defined arrays in a simple way and now it is time to know them and know how they work. Arrays are a variable and this variable contains more than one value or element and each element has an index. This index starts from zero if you do not specify it.

Example :

```
<?
$ A [] = "alfareees";
$ A [] = 13;
?>
```

In this example, the PHP will automatically give indexing.

```
$ A [0] = "alfareees";
$ A [1] = 13;
```

We did not enter these numbers by ourselves, but PHP put them in, although we can enter them normally. For example, if we write:

```
<?
$ A [0] = "alfareees";
$ A [1] = 13;
?>
```

PHP will take the indexed and will not put any other indexing We can also write any indexing and do not rely on the order in the numbers.

Example :

```
<?
$ A [10] = "alfareees";
$ A [25] = 13;
?>
```

Did you also notice that we did not define the type of matrix variables and PHP defined automatically instead of us once we used a literal value and once we used a number and yet PHP did not make any objection In addition, the PHP determines the number of elements of the array automatically. Elements of the macro matrix is two elements.

PHP gives us another advantage, which is not to restrict numbers in indexing. For example, we can use regular characters.

Example :

```
<?
$ A ["a"] = "alfareees";
$ A ["b"] = 13;
?>
```

Note that we used literal values and PHPJ never intercepted and we could simply print any element of the array.

Example :

```
<?
$ r ["aa"] = "ahmed ali";
$ r [1] = 13273;
$ r [20] = 13273;
echo $ r [aa];
echo $ r [20];
echo $ r ["aa"];
?>
```

There is no difference between writing aa (aa) between quotation marks when typing and when typing without quotes ... PHP will know this automatically.

We can also define matrices in another way

```
$ variable = array (elements);
```

Example :

```
<?
$ t = array ("ahmed", "ali", "salem", "alfarsi");
echo $ t [0];
?>
```

The PHP gives each element of the array an index number, which is as follows:

Element

Ahmed 0

Ali 1

Salem 2

alfarsi 3

So the value that PHP will print at the end is ahmed.Note that PHP gave the index number and started from zero, but we can make PHP start indexing from one number as follows:

```
<?
$ r = array (1 => "ahmed", "ali", "salem", "alfarsi");
?>
```

When you define the index number for the first value, PHP will give index numbers sequentially,

The index will then read:

Element

ahmed 1

Ali 2

salem 3

alfarsi 4

There is a way to also be indexing is by capital letters:

<?

$ r = array ("ss" => "ahmed", "sf" => "ali", "da" => "salem", "bv" => "alfarsi");

?>

The index will then read:

Element

Ahmed Ss

Ali Sf

Salem Da

Alfarsi Bv

When we want to change any element in an array, we can do it simply.

Example :

$ r [ss] = "Lamia";

Note that we have changed the value from (ahmed) to (Lamia) .... simple way is not it:)

Read arrays and extract values

We talked earlier about repetition

We can extract matrix elements and print them in simplicity and save time by duplicates

Suppose you have this matrix:

```
<?
$ people = array ("ahmed", "ali", "salem", "alfarsi");
?>
```


I wanted to print the names of all the people in it

First, we know that if we do not define an array index, PHP starts indexing it from zero, so the first element number 0 and the fourth element number 3 ... So we can simply write the following code that prints the array as follows:

```
<?
$ people = array ("ahmed", "ali", "salem", "alfarsi");
echo "$ people [0]. <br> ";
echo "$ people [1]. <br> ";
echo "$ people [2]. <br> ";
echo "$ people [3]. <br> ";
?>
```

Suppose you have thirty or three thousand names in a matrix because this method looks a little tiring !!!

Another way is through duplicates.

Suppose we want to write a repetition that prints numbers from one to ten, we can write the repetition as follows:

```
<?
For ($ I = 1; $ I <11; $ I ++)
{
Echo "$ I <br>";
}
?>
```

Now let's say we want to print the four elements in the array.

```
<?
$ people = array ("ahmed", "ali", "salem", "alfarsi");

For ($ I = 0; $ I <4; $ I ++)
{
Echo "$ people [$ I] <br>";
}
?>
```

Notice that we started the counter with a value of zero and then we set it to be less than 4 because the last element in the array indexed number 3 and then we made it increase by 1 because we want to print all elements of the array and we put the counter number in the indexing box and so will be in each repeating the matrix element that Its index is equal to the counter number.

Previously, in the model lesson we talked about removing values from a matrix list.

Example :

<form action = "array.php" method = post>

what is your favorite drink ?

<select name = "a []" multiple>

<option> Tea </option>

<option> Coffee </option>

<option> Cappuccino </option>

<option> Tut </option>

<option> Orange </option>

</select>

<input type = submit value = "Delicious">

</form>

In the array.php file, type:

```
<html>

You have selected the following:

<?

For ($ l = 0; $ l <4; $ l ++)

{

Echo "$ a [$ l] <br>";

}

?>

</html>
```

We have listed five elements in the list ... Note that we put in the variable name in parentheses [] so that the html recognizes that the data will be stored automatically after that the PHP indexed the elements sent by the client, whether three or four, but of course will not exceed Five .... so the last digit ending in the matrix would be 4.

I expect you are now starting to like matrices .... we can make the list through the matrix as well ....

Example :

```
<form action = "list.php" method = post>

what is your favorite drink ?
```

```
<br>

<select name = "s">

<?

$ shrab = array ("Tea", "Coffee", "Cappuccino", "Raspberry", "Orange");

For ($ k = 0; $ k <4; $ k ++)

{

echo "<option>". $ shrab [$ k]. "</option>";

}

?>

</select>

</form>
```

When the user selects the value, it will be placed in the variable $ s. Build a list that will build a list that will contain these states by matrices and iterations.

Save the changes in the php extension file and write the list.php file based on your previous information in the sample lesson.

Array functions

Function key

Suppose we have a matrix of two elements:

Example :

$ s = array ("محمد" ,"علی");

Now let's add to these lines

<?

$ s = array ("محمد" ,"علی");

$ t = key ($ s);

echo $ t;

?>

The key command finds the index number (index) of the currently active element .... the number is zero since we did not index and this is the indexing that PHP automatically set when we did not index ... Later .

Indexing number may be letters or words

Example :

<?

$ s = array ("محمد" <= "م" ,"علی" <= "ع");

$ t = key ($ s);

echo $ t;

?>

Current () function

The current function finds the value of the current array element (index value).

Example :

```
<?
$ s = array ("محمد" => "م" , "علی" <= "ع");
$ p = current ($ s);
echo $ p;
?>
```

In the previous example, we found the current value of the active object ....
Notice that we created the index key number command while the current
command found the value of the indexed object.

How do we activate the other elements of the matrix ?!

We can do this by the next () and prev functions, which are navigating
between the elements of the array ... Suppose we have an array of three
elements

Example :

```
<?
$ s = array ("احمد" <= "ا" , "محمد" <= "م" , "علی" <= "ع");
echo key ($ s). "<br>";
echo current ($ s). "<br>";
?>
```

In this example, we have printed the value of the index number of the
current element and its value (the index number means the letter (p) and I
mean the value (on) .... Let's now navigate between the elements of the
array and let's see the result of printing.

Example :

```
<?
$ s = array ("احمد" => "١" ,"محمد" => "م" ,"على" => "ع");
next ($ s);
echo key ($ s). "<br>";
echo current ($ s). "<br>";
?>
```


```
<?
$ s = array ("احمد" => "١" ,"محمد" => "م" ,"على" => "ع");
next ($ s);
next ($ s);
echo key ($ s). "<br>";
echo current ($ s). "<br>";
?>
```

Note that we wrote the next () function before moving on to activate the second element in the first example and to activate the third element in the third example (note that we wrote the next () twice).

We can go back to activate the previous element by placing the prev () function. For example, we can modify the following example:

```
<?
$ s = array (" => "١" ,"محمد" => "م" ,"على" => "ع");
next ($ s);
```

```php
next ($ s);

prev ($ s);

echo key ($ s). "<br>";

echo current ($ s). "<br>";

?>
```

PHP in this case will print the second element, not the third because the step has been undone by prev ()

What will happen if we add an element on an unlimited indexing matrix ?!

Suppose we have an array and we add an unspecified indexing element to it. Like :

```php
<?

$ s = array (12 => "احمد" <= 44 ,"محمد" <= 5 ,"علی");

$ s [] = "هشام";

Next ($ s);

Next ($ s);

Next ($ s);

Echo key ($ s). "<br>";

Echo current ($ s). "<br>";

?>
```


The PHP will simply search for the largest index number and then begin to give the index a sequence after it. If the index numbers are letters starting from zero in the number given .. Notice in this example that he gave the element number 45 because the largest element in the matrix is 44 and therefore gave Sequence after this number.

The List and Each function

Suppose you have created an array that is not indexed in order

Example :

```
<?
$ s = array (12 => "احمد" <= 44 ,"محمد" <= 5 ,"على");
?>
```

So let us tell you a good news that you can make your PHP life easier with your life with yourself!

While (list (Index, Element value) = each (array)

With these functions and by repetition while you can extract all the elements in the array

```
While (list ($ e, $ r) = each ($ s))
{
echo "<br> $ e <br> $ r";
}
```

First, you name two variables, one of which is for the index number ($ e) and the second for the item ($ r) and we can name them by any name. If we only want to display the item or know the item, we can delete ($ e)

```
While (list (, $ r) = each ($ s))
{
echo "<br> $ e <br> $ r";
}
```

Let's go back to the example where the index number and element ...
Repeat will put the index number (which may be text) in the variable $ e
and put the value of the item that the index number is $ e in the variable $
r and then print the elements until all of them are finished. .

Important note: If you do not define an index for the array (whatever
letters or numbers), the elements are used when the iteration requests the
indexes.

Example :

```
<?

$ e = array ("fsda", "terhfgfd", "tewr");

While (list ($ I, $ V) = each ($ e))

{

echo "<br> $ e [$ I]";

}

?>
```

Note with H that we asked to print index, but the elements were taken
instead of indexing

With this function, we can make useful things. As an example, suppose we
have a phone number matrix and we want to get this matrix on an html
table.

Example :

```
<table align = 'center' dir = "rtl" border = "1" width = "100%" cellspacing =
"0" bordercolorlight = "# 000000" bordercolordark = "# 000000"
```

Printed in Great Britain
by Amazon

34813923R00073